Seven Tales
of Vice and Virtue

by JSB Morse

Pierre Fierre Loses a Dare! 2

(Pride and Humility)

Little Dragons 13

(Sloth and Diligence)

Ava Rice Gets Something Nice! 23

(Greed and Charity)

The Adventures of Ziggy Wigglefuzz 33

(Lust and Chastity)

The Squirrels Go Nuts! 45

(Envy and Kindness)

Popino 55

(Gluttony and Temperence)

Princess Eloise Learns to Say Please 65

(Wrath and Meekness)

Copyright © 2024 by JSB Morse. All Rights Reserved. Printed in the United States of America.

This book was produced by Libertas Kids, an imprint of Code Publishing, Covington, LA. LibertasKids.com
ISBN Hardcover: 978-1-60020-134-9 Paperback: 978-1-60020-136-3 Ebook: 978-1-60020-135-6

Pierre Fierre Loses a Dare!

Deep in the bayou where the swamp meets the land,
King Pierre Fierre ruled with an iron hand.
For he was the biggest, the strongest, and best,
His roars echoed loudly when he beat on his chest.
Every day he made all his subjects sing a hymn,
And begrudgingly they all lifted their voices for him.

Hail King Pierre Fierre, with power and pomp,
The most handsomest beast who ever lived in the swamp.
With bumps and ridges on your tail so grand,
You make us so proud to live in your land.

With a noble snout and a stately jaw,
And regal talons that leave us in awe.
Oh King Pierre Fierre, so grand and so strong,
We're so honored to slave for you all day long.

He'd dance and he'd strut, oh, so full of pride,
As he marched by his subjects with an arrogant stride.

But one little creature, a turtle named Beau,
Decided he'd had enough of the show.
So, he turned his back on the song and dance,
And that startled the others right out of their trance.

Pierre saw this slight and he let out a shout.
"How dare you not worship your master, you lout!?"
Beau said, "Sorry I won't worship or sing,
For I only bow to the one and true King."
"Hey, I am the ruler of this here swamp, Beau.
Sing for me T, or I'll make you into gumbo!"

Beau pondered his choices, a weight on his chest,
Should he sing with the others or put courage to test?
But the gator was too big and he had no chance,
So he put a foot forward and started to dance.
Pierre laughed. "That's better kid. That's how it should be.
All of my subjects must always praise me!"

That night under the moon's silvery gleam,
Beau gathered the animals to hatch up a scheme.
He spoke with conviction in the humid night air,
"Let's unite together and overthrow Pierre!"

But the animals all scoffed, "There's just no way, Beau.
Pierre's just too strong, from his snout to his toe."
Beau shook his head, "There must be a way,"
And then, Evangeline, the owl, had her say.

"Pierre is mighty, but he's prouder than all,
And pride, as they say, goes before the fall.
Beau's right there's a way. I have seen it from the air.
With help from above we can get rid of Pierre!"
So the animals worked together to come up with a plan,
To overthrow the despot and bring peace to the land.

The next morning everyone lined up ready to sing,
Except for little Beau, defying the king.
Pierre grinned wide at the treacherous sight.
"So, I guess it's turtle soup for breakfast, all right!"
Beau said, "Wait a minute there, Tyrannosaur!
Before you eat me, may I please have the floor?"

"You think you're so marvelous and big and smart,
But you have no compassion, no guts, and no heart!"
"I challenge you to a race," Beau declared with some flair,
"To that hill with the sign over there if you dare."

"No thanks," said Pierre, "I'll just eat you right here."
"What's the matter?" asked Beau. "Do I smell fear?"
Pierre chuckled with a quick and sly grin,
"All right, I'll race you, but don't think you'll win!
This isn't some fable and I ain't no hare,
I'm the fastest and smartest. I'm Pierre Fierre!"

The lightning bugs signaled the start of the race,
And Pierre tore off leaving Beau in his wake.
They raced to the sign, Pierre won, it was clear,
And everyone was quiet so he made them all cheer.

As they cheered for their king, in the midst of their hymn,
The creatures stopped singing and just stared at him.
"What's the matter, Cher?" Pierre asked with a frown,
When hunters with a snare and a net took him down.

Pierre Fierre, the swamp's once-mighty king,
Was taken and thrown into a circus ring.
They made him the butt of a joke for the crowd,
And Pierre learned the price of being so proud.
For everyone who exalts himself will be low,
And he should've been kinder to his subjects and Beau.

And Beau, the turtle, so meek and so small,
Had proven that pride causes the mighty to fall.
All the animals said, "For Beau, we'll now sing!"
But Beau said, "No, for God is the King."

THE END.

"Pride goeth before destruction,
And a haughty spirit before a fall." - Proverbs 16:18

Little Dragons

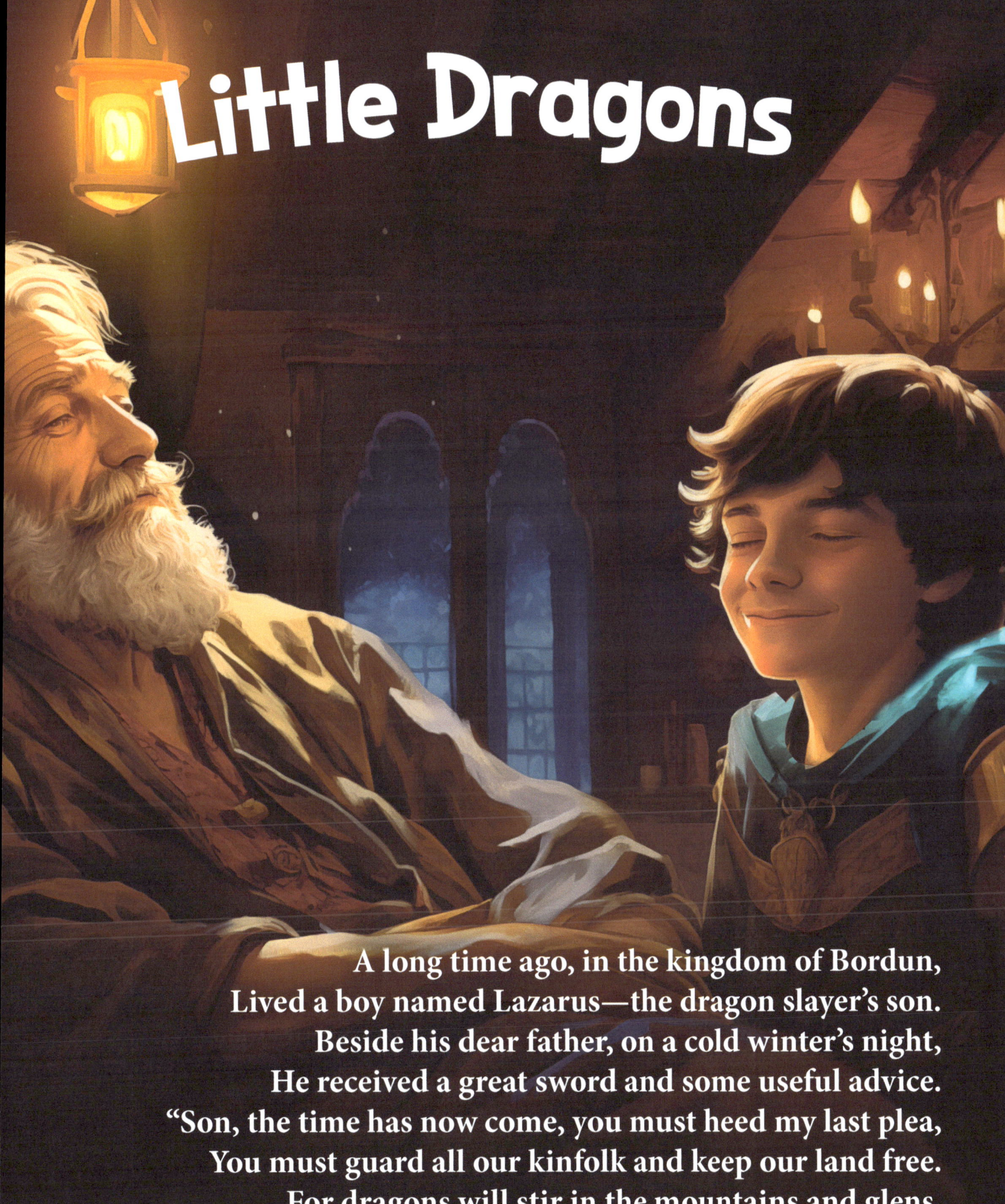

A long time ago, in the kingdom of Bordun,
Lived a boy named Lazarus—the dragon slayer's son.
Beside his dear father, on a cold winter's night,
He received a great sword and some useful advice.
"Son, the time has now come, you must heed my last plea,
You must guard all our kinfolk and keep our land free.
For dragons will stir in the mountains and glens,
And you are the only hope to defend against them."

"You'll take my own sword, with courage and might,
To slay all the dragons and stand for what's right.
You're the last in the line of slayers, it's true,
The fate of our village now depends all on you."
But the young dragon slayer was tired and lazy.
Instead of picking up swords he'd rather pick daisies.
While others would toil in the sun's hot, hot rays,
Lazarus snoozed in a bale of soft hay.

His favorite thing to do was lay in his hammock,
And gaze into the medieval panoramic.
He'd linger and wait and he'd pause and delay,
A master of putting things off for the day.
The townspeople begged, their voices sincere,
"You must go slay the dragons that keep us in fear!"
"I'll do it tomorrow," Lazarus would say,
But the villagers pleaded and urged him and begged.

So, reluctantly the young dragon slayer agreed,
And slowly he marched off to do his sworn deed.
He tried to think up a way out of the job,
So he wouldn't have to go deal with the mob.
If only those dragons would all fly away,
He could go back home and sleep through the day.

When he got to the lair, he saw dragons all right,
But they were all tiny and none of them could fight.
One bit his finger; they weren't very nice.
But they were so small they couldn't harm a fly.

Relieved he said, "I'll go home and get some rest,
These dragons are harmless and no cause for stress."
Lazarus was glad he didn't have to fight,
And he left them in peace and went home for the night.
With wicked grins the dragons waved him off.
For they knew they'd been spared by the dragon slayer's sloth.

The next day he calmed all the villagers' fears.
"Those dragons aren't a threat and won't be for years."
"So you slayed them?" a villager expectantly asked.
Not knowing what to do, he lied and said, "Uhhh yeah."

Months passed by, as they often tend to do,
With nary a thought of the dragons, it's true.
The young lad grew older and lazier each day,
He didn't want to work and just wanted to play.

One day Lazarus lay in his hammock bed,
When a fair maiden ran up to him and said:
"The dragons are back, you must stand up to them all!"
He scoffed, "But I told you Miss, those dragons are small!"

But his smile quickly turned to a horrified frown,
When he looked up to a fully-grown beast swooping down.
With wings that stretched wide, and teeth shining bright,
It towered above him—a terrible sight.

He realized something, albeit too late,
That problems, unaddressed, can ruin one's fate.
The dragons ruthlessly scorched the whole village.
They destroyed and wrecked and they broke and pillaged.
In a blazing inferno, they turned it all to ash;
That once lively hamlet was destroyed in a flash.

So, let this be a lesson to know,
That dragons start small but those dragons can grow.
Too much rest or slumber or sleep,
And misery will strike like a beast.

THE END.

"The hand of the diligent shall bear rule;
But the slothful shall be put under taskwork." - Proverbs 12:24

Ava Rice Gets Something Nice!

In a land not far away, there lived a girl named Ava Rice,
Who had a love for money, her heart's only vice.
She'd steal from her brothers, hoarding coins galore.
She dreamed of being the richest and always wanting more.

One sunny day, Ava's grandpa came to town,
With a gift for the girl, both strange and profound.
The box had the shape of a 20-pound bean,
And it had odd writing on it, like nothing she'd seen.

Grandpa said "This box holds immeasurable worth,
In fact, it holds the greatest treasure on Earth!"
And the treasure was hers if she could open the box,
But she had to be clever to unlock the locks.

Ava tried everything, from saws to a hammer,
But the box wouldn't budge despite all the clamor.
It stayed tightly shut and Ava became irate,
So, she kicked it and smashed it with her mom's finest plate.

Then Ava had an idea: to decipher the text!
She researched old languages, feeling quite perplexed.
But learned it was Aramaic, a language of old,
And discovered the message that the box writing told.

The message on the box was clear and true,
"Give, and it shall be given to you."
A biblical lesson, so simple and sound,
It was like a golden rule that Ava had found.
She contemplated the message with a thoughtful stare,
Aware of her greed, a weight she couldn't bear.

With remorse in her heart, she would right her wrongs,
Return what she had taken and mend all the bonds.
At first it was hard to part with her cash.
When she spent it on others her teeth would all gnash.
But as time went on, she liked this new way of living,
She discovered the real joy in cheerfully giving.
She gave a nice toy to each of her brothers,
And she replaced that fine plate she'd destroyed of her mother's.

Then she branched out with her gift-giving grace,
To a friend, a kind word and a smile on her face.
Then she gave a hand to an old lady in need,
Spreading love and compassion and goodwill indeed.

Then magically the box opened up with a click,
So Ava rushed over to look inside quick.
She had given to others so she would receive,
At least that's what the box led her to believe.

Ava looked inside the box with hope in her eyes,
But it was totally empty, to her sad surprise.

Inside the box was nothing at all,
She wanted to cry and she wanted to bawl.
Confronting her grandpa, she exclaimed, "You lied to me!
This just isn't right; it's not how it should be!"

Her grandpa just smiled and nodded his head,
And took her in his arms and he lovingly said,
"My dear, my dear, all that glitters isn't gold,
Your kindness is worth more than anything that's sold."

"You've learned the value of giving without measure,
For giving with love is the world's greatest treasure.
True wealth lies not in the riches one can see,
But in kindness and giving and in charity."

With a smile and a hug and a wink of his eye,
He turned to leave and gave a, "Goodbye!"
Ava said, "thank you" for the lesson she now knew,
But as he left with a smile, he said, "No, no, thank *you*."

THE END.

"Give, and it shall be given unto you." - Luke 6:38

The Adventures of Ziggy Wigglefuzz

In the most magical land that ever was,
Lived a brave young boy named Ziggy Wigglefuzz.
At ten years old, he began his quest,
To go fight for the king and be truly blessed.
His father gave him a medallion so bright,
With the family crest and a guiding light.
"Guard it well, Son," his father did say,
"Without it, you won't get past the castle gate!

With that he set off for the castle so grand,
When he saw his friends going to Ninnypig Land.
"Come with us!" they said, "You don't want to miss it!
You can do what you want there, you just have to visit!"
But Ziggy said, "No, I'm going to fight for the king."
His friends all laughed and their laughter did sting.

"Well," he thought, "Ninnypig Land is on the way.
It wouldn't hurt to go there a while and play.
So, he went and he played and he had so much fun,
Acting like animals out in the sun.

But Ziggy knew that he couldn't stay,
That he had to be off and on his way.
"I have to get going or else I'll be late,
In two hours I should be at the castle gate!"

His friends wanted him to stay in Ninnypig Land,
But he left with haste and medallion in hand.
His friend Oliver Wobblepants came too,
And off they marched under sky so blue.

When all at once a woman approached them,
And offered them glowing candies like gems.
They wanted to say no to the prize in her fists,
But they were so mesmerized, they couldn't resist.

But the candies made them feel like fools.
They ate and they ate but they never got full.
Still they asked for more because it looked so great,
But she said, "No, you owe me for what you already ate!"
But Ziggy and Oliver didn't have a dime,
So she said, "Then you must work for it in my coal mine!"

It was a trick by the nice-looking witch.
The glowing blue candy was a bait and switch.
So, into the coal mine the two boys were led,
To work like slaves to pay off their debt.
They toiled for days in the dusty mine,
Regretting their choice, they groaned and they whined.

When along came a man named Silas Shadowbane,
Who said he could take away all of their pain.
"You don't have to work as animals like this,
You could be having fun in eternal bliss!
I'll show you a way down a magical cave,
With all the Glimmer Gum you could ever crave!"

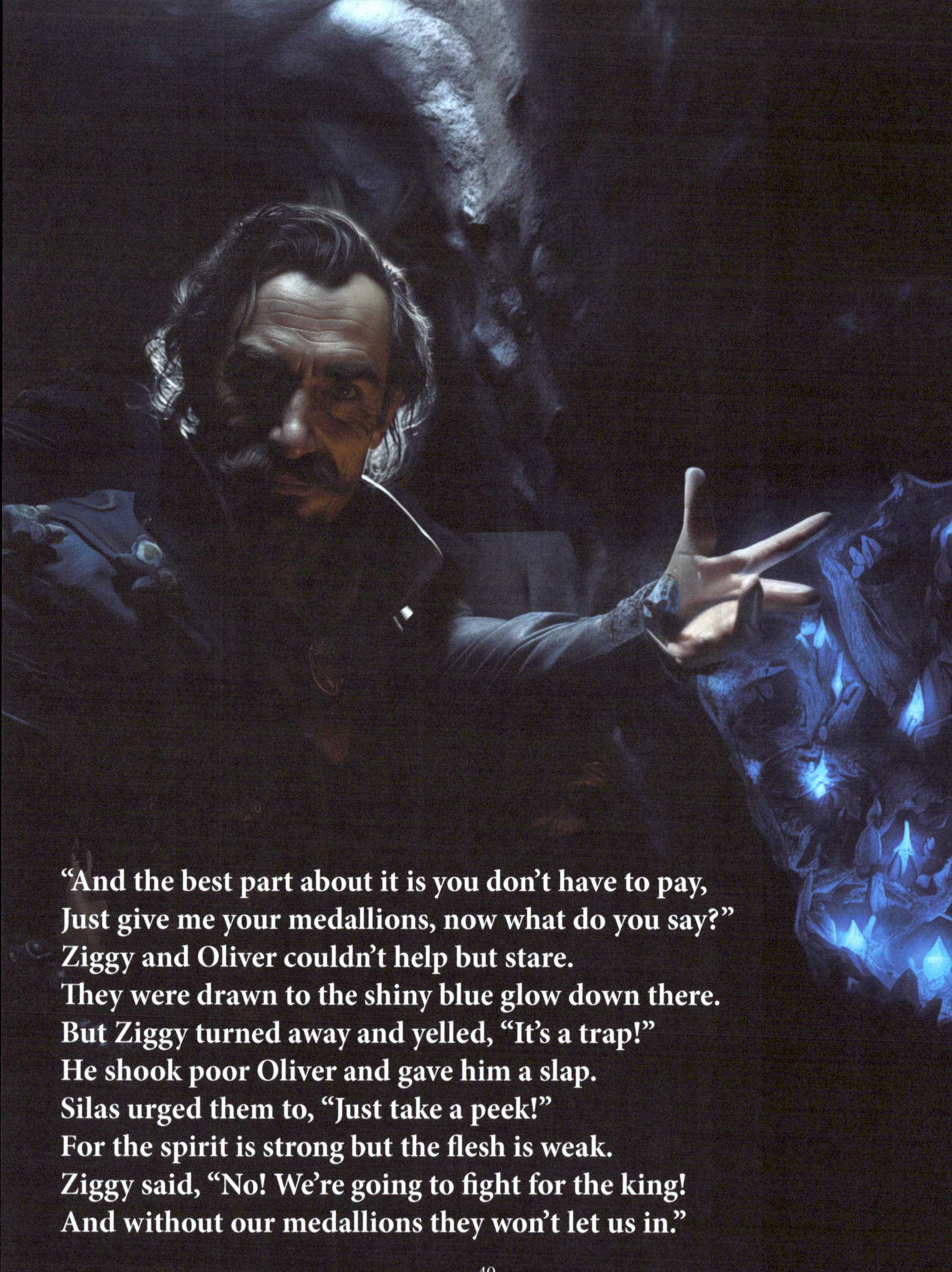

"And the best part about it is you don't have to pay,
Just give me your medallions, now what do you say?"
Ziggy and Oliver couldn't help but stare.
They were drawn to the shiny blue glow down there.
But Ziggy turned away and yelled, "It's a trap!"
He shook poor Oliver and gave him a slap.
Silas urged them to, "Just take a peek!"
For the spirit is strong but the flesh is weak.
Ziggy said, "No! We're going to fight for the king!
And without our medallions they won't let us in."

"Suit yourselves," said Silas with a weak little wave,
Then he turned back to crawl down his magical cave.
But Oliver was hooked on the dazzling glow,
Completely ignoring the toll he would owe.
Ziggy tried everything to stop his good friend,
But Oliver screamed and smacked Ziggy's head.
So sadly Ziggy left behind his best mate,
A victim of lustrous glowing blue bait.

He toiled for days to pay off what he owed,
Then he hiked back up to the castle road.
As he got closer he was amazed at the majesty,
But was sad it wasn't something Oliver could see.
At the gate he was greeted by guards so valiant,
And he smiled when he showed them his shining medallion.
The gates opened and lo and behold...

Oliver stood there all dressed in gold!
"But how?" Ziggy asked, "I thought you fell in the cave!"
"I was going to, yeah, but then I was saved!"

"Just before I got there I called out to the king,
And along came this luminous messenger thing.
It lifted me out of the deep and dark pit,
And brought me straight to the castle with it."

"That's wonderful!" Ziggy exclaimed with a cheer,
"I'm so happy that both of us made it up here!"
And together they went to receive their swords,
To train and to fight for their righteous Lord.

THE END.

"Watch and pray, that ye enter not into temptation: the spirit indeed is willing, but the flesh is weak." - Matthew 26:41

The Squirrels Go Nuts!

Once upon a time in a wood so fair,
A community of squirrels lived without care.
They gathered their nuts and saved them right,
And everyone slept quite soundly at night.
But one fateful day, a chipmunk named Red,
Came to their town and filled them with dread.

He pointed out squirrels who kept nuts in excess,
Creating envy among the squirrels who had less.
"Look at them hoarding, it just isn't fair!
We must share all our nuts to show how we care!"

The squirrels listened, their hearts filled with doubt.
Could sharing their nuts truly even things out?
They agreed to Red's plan, their faith he had won,
And together they gathered nuts by the ton.

They hid them away in a common store,
Then hibernated, to sleep and to snore.
But Red stayed awake, with a mischievous grin,
He ate all their nuts, committing a terrible sin.

In Spring they awoke with rumbling tummies,
They scurried around in search of their yummies.
But alas, no nuts could they find anywhere,
Their bellies all grumbled, empty and bare.

Confusion filled the air, their tummies felt hollow,
No nuts to be found, a sight hard to swallow.
They looked at each other, their faces dismayed,
As the truth slowly dawned, their hearts felt betrayed.

Red, the sly chipmunk, pointed with glee,
Blaming poor Gray, shouting "It was he!"
"Gray took our nuts!" Red loudly exclaimed,
Filling the squirrels' hearts with anger and blame.

Gray tried to explain, with a voice so meek,
"I was hibernating then, so it couldn't have been me!"
But Red interjected, with a wicked grin,
"Gray always hoarded more, so clearly it was him!"
Envy clouded the squirrels' judgment and sight,
And they banish poor Gray, a victim of spite.

Distrust spread like wildfire, fueling their fears,
And the squirrels wondered this while holding back tears,
Who would be banished, who would be next?
Their suspicion and distrust had them all vexed.
They pretended to bury their nuts on the sly,
To catch other thieving squirrels passing by.
But little did they know, their plan would backfire,
As their mistrust of others rose higher and higher.

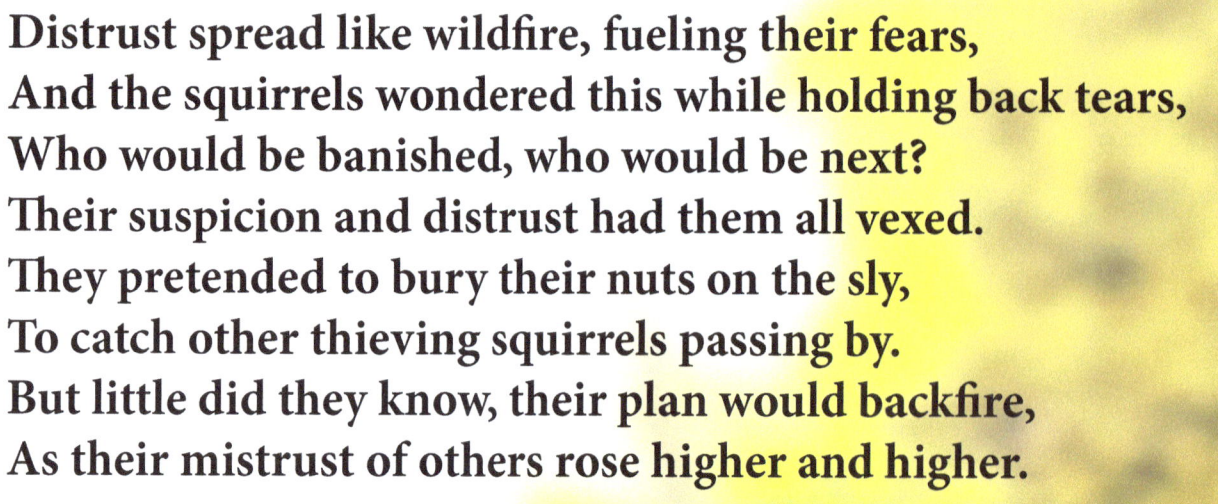

And when fall arrived, lazy squirrels abound,
They ate what they saw and kept nothing they found.
They disregarded the need to store for the cold,
Unaware of the hunger that soon would unfold.
And so the harvest that fall was incredibly small.
Red got angry and yelled, "Are you kidding? Is that all?!"

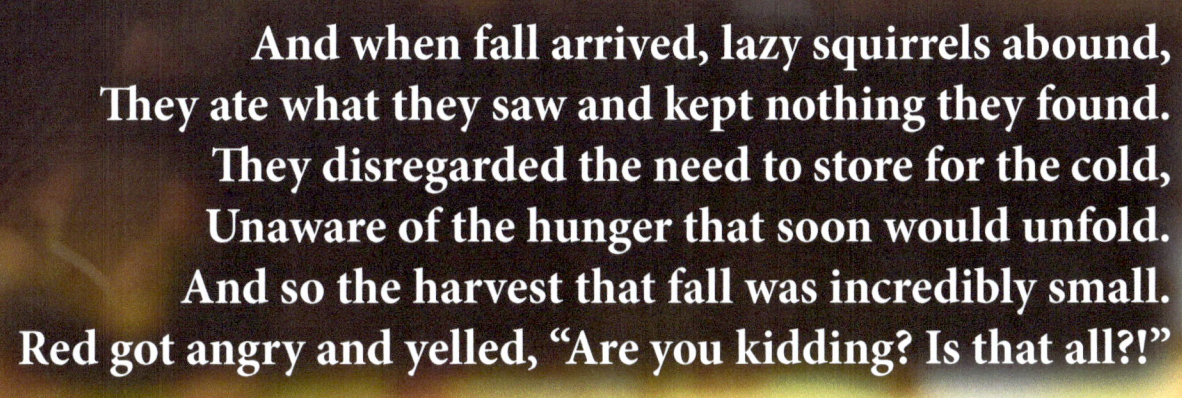

As the winter arrived, they settled to rest,
Hibernating squirrels, hoping for the best.
In their dreams, visions of nuts filled their minds,
Counting on the plenty they hoped they would find.

But when spring came again, their shock was profound,
Someone had stolen their nuts—every pound!
All of their hopes and desires had turned to despair,
The commons were empty with no nuts to share!

Red pointed his paw, accusing a squirrel named Blue,
But the others saw through his lies, oh they knew.
They caught Red red-handed with crumbs on his nose,
The devious chipmunk had reached the lowest of lows.

With swift action, the squirrels showed Red the door,
No longer deceived by his tricks anymore.
They threw the chipmunk out of the wood,
And welcomed back dear old Gray for good.
The squirrels learned a lesson that was both wise and true:
It's not what others have that should matter to you.
Inequality may hurt and envy it may stoke,
But it's infinitely better than being equally broke.

Mandating charity led to envy and strife,
But taking responsibility brought abundant life.
They returned to their old way of peacefully living,
Where each squirrel takes only what he's giving.
And they lived happily ever after in the peaceful wood,
Being happy for others and wishing their good.

THE END.

"Then I saw that all toil and all skill in work come from one person's envy of another. This also is vanity and a chasing after wind." - Ecclesiastes 4:4

Popino

In a leafy perch so high and so bendy,
Lived Popino, a bird with cravings aplenty.
While his flock all nibbled on nature's delights,
Popino always wanted a much bigger bite.
His parents warned him of the perils he faced,
"Too much junk and it'll just end up on your waist!
We are migrating soon to the Southern skies.
Keep eating like that and you won't be able to fly!"

Popino cried out as he lifted a wing,
"But I just love food more than anything!"
"I know but it's just not healthy or right,
To eat everything you see all day and all night."
They took all the snacks he was mindlessly crunching,
And they hid them away to stop him from munching.

Papa Bird warned, "And sneaking food? Don't even try it!"
I know you were thinking that, don't you deny it!"
Popino turned away, humming, "You don't understand!"
And he flew down from the branch to hatch up a plan.

For he knew that in the house there nearby,
They were cooking up dozens of Thanksgiving pies!
He flew around to look for a way in,
Then he saw an opening beckoning him.
He flew up and in and saw a marvelous sight,
An amazing feast of Thanksgiving delights!

And so he indulged his huge appetite,
Devouring not one, not two, but three pies!
But he ate so fast, he didn't even enjoy them,
Then he heard people coming so he ran to avoid them.

There was a problem; he chirped and he coughed.
He had eaten so much that he couldn't take off!
He hopped and he flopped—oh so full of pie,
He needed to leave but he couldn't fly!

"Who ate the desserts!?" the angry homeowner screamed.
Then he looked and saw the fattest bird he'd ever seen.
"You!" And he grabbed the nearest weapon he could,
Then he swung and he hit and he broke his hardwood.
He struck a plate that launched Popino in the air,
Sending him through the window on a wing and a prayer.

Popino awoke the next morning dazed and dim,
And he saw his flock flying South without him.
"Wait for me!" he shouted as he tried to fly,
But he couldn't, so he watched and just whispered,
"Good bye…"

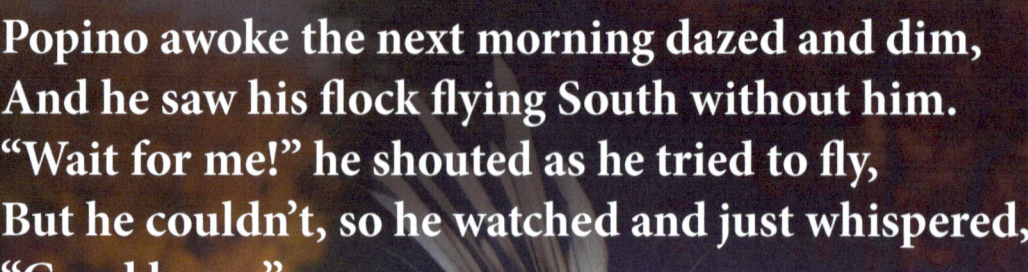

A freezing north wind reminded him he couldn't linger.
He had to get moving and walk South for the winter.
So he started his long cold walk to the South,
With none of his friends or family about.
Ashamed and lonely, with feathers so cold,
If only he had listened to the lesson he was told.

He started to cry little sparrow tears,
When down flew his papa, erasing his fears.
"You came back for me?" Popino hopefully asked,
His dad said, "My son, I never left you, in fact."

Papa bird explained, with wisdom so true,
"I was watching all along, though it hurt me to.
Letting a child fail is the hardest thing to do,
But sometimes it's the only way for a lesson to get through.

It's not that we don't want you happy, we do,
But being ruled by your stomach just isn't good for you.
There's one thing that we wish you would know:
That one cannot live on bread alone.

"Your little body is a temple of the Holy Ghost,
So you must be careful what you shove down your throat!"
God gave you the amazing gift of flight.
Control yourself and you'll reach endless heights.

So with Papa, Popino set off for the South,
Being much more careful what he put in his mouth.
Papa showed him the pleasures of eating naturally,
Gathering nuts and fall berries, as happy as can be.

And after a few days of walking, Popino was able to fly.
He lifted off and soared up, up into the sky.
He vowed never again to be stuck on the ground,
And with the sky as his limit, his life knew no bounds.

THE END.

"Your body is a temple of the Holy Spirit which is in you, which ye have from God." - 1 Corinthians 6:19-20

Princess Eloise Learns to Say Please

In the Snuggle Wump Kingdom lived Princess Eloise,
With a joyful giggle when she got what she pleased.
For the young princess had kindness galore,
But only when she got all that she asked for.
As her birthday drew near, she jumped up and down,
"I want to go see the magical Glow Trees in town!"

King Thaddeus frowned, shaking his head,
"But there are Gobble Groks out there," he said.
"They're monsters with teeth that are jagged and long,
With eyes that glow brightly and claws sharp and strong.
They gobble up children and princesses too,
So staying inside is what you must do."

Eloise's sweet smile turned into a frown,
And soon her whole face was turned upside down.
She stomped and she screamed, she hollered and spat,
The castle walls trembled from the tantruming brat.
The King, looking weary, sent her to her room,
But that only made it worse and filled the castle with doom.
She yelled and she cried, till the stars filled the night,
And fell into sleep with her heart full of spite.

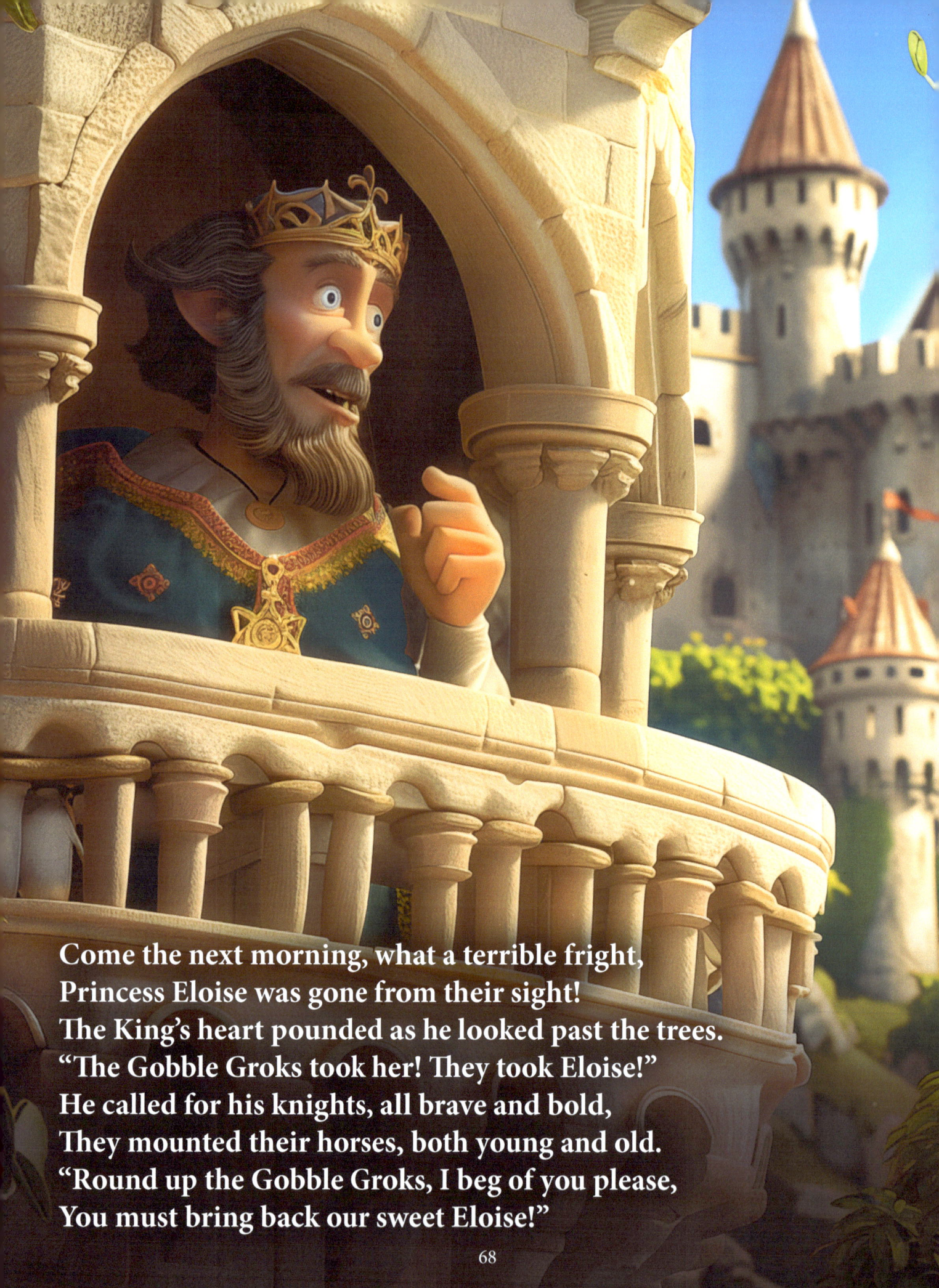

Come the next morning, what a terrible fright,
Princess Eloise was gone from their sight!
The King's heart pounded as he looked past the trees.
"The Gobble Groks took her! They took Eloise!"
He called for his knights, all brave and bold,
They mounted their horses, both young and old.
"Round up the Gobble Groks, I beg of you please,
You must bring back our sweet Eloise!"

They posted signs that read, "Princess missing. Huge reward,
For anyone who saves her from the barbarian horde!"
Through forests so dark, through shadows and night,
They searched for the princess with all of their might.

But the knights couldn't find their dear Princess Eloise,
Though they found several Gobble Groks lurking in trees.
They chased and they captured all of the Groks,
Then threw them all into a cage with a lock.

The King addressed them: "You rancorous slugs!
You took my daughter, you overgrown bugs.
If you haven't gobbled her yet, hear my plea,
Return our dear Eloise, and I'll set you free."

The Groks just yelled and jumped around in their cage,
A bunch of fools giving vent to their rage.
Then the King saw one Grok gnawing a shoe,
Wearing a tiara, he asked, "Darling, that you?"
The Grok turned red and embarrassed as can be.
"Yes, Papa, it is me. Your darling Eloise.
The Gobble Groks didn't kidnap or take me.
I got so mad last night that I became one, you see?"

Everyone was horrified, grossed out, and shocked,
To hear that their sweet princess had turned into a Grok.
But the King nodded and said, "I must tell you,
A long time ago, I turned into a Grok too."

"And I nearly did again just now, it's true,
It's horrible, but there's a way to turn you back into you.
If you don't like being a Grok, there's a way to change you back,
But it's going to take work to get you back on track."

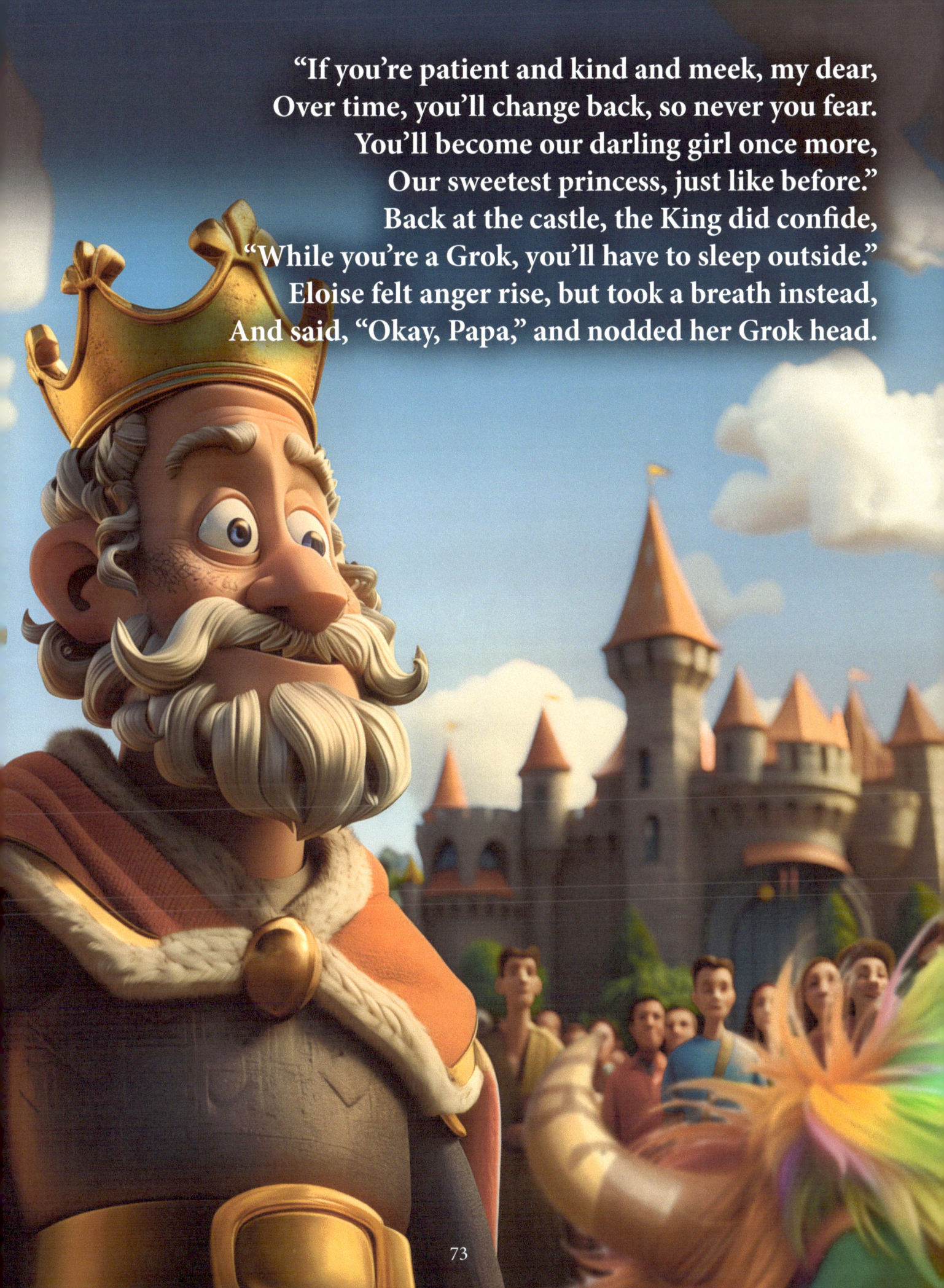

"If you're patient and kind and meek, my dear,
Over time, you'll change back, so never you fear.
You'll become our darling girl once more,
Our sweetest princess, just like before."
Back at the castle, the King did confide,
"While you're a Grok, you'll have to sleep outside."
Eloise felt anger rise, but took a breath instead,
And said, "Okay, Papa," and nodded her Grok head.

And when she didn't like her food one bit,
She ate it all and did not throw a fit.
Eloise started saying thank you every day,
And helped around the castle in many small ways.

The princess practiced meekness with care,
In her humble deeds with kindness to share.
She listened to others and gave of her time,
With a heart so gentle, her spirit began to shine.

Then on her birthday she asked again to see the trees,
And again the King said, "No," to the Grok Eloise,
But she didn't throw a fit or even yell or scream.
She did what every child should do and simply said, "Please."

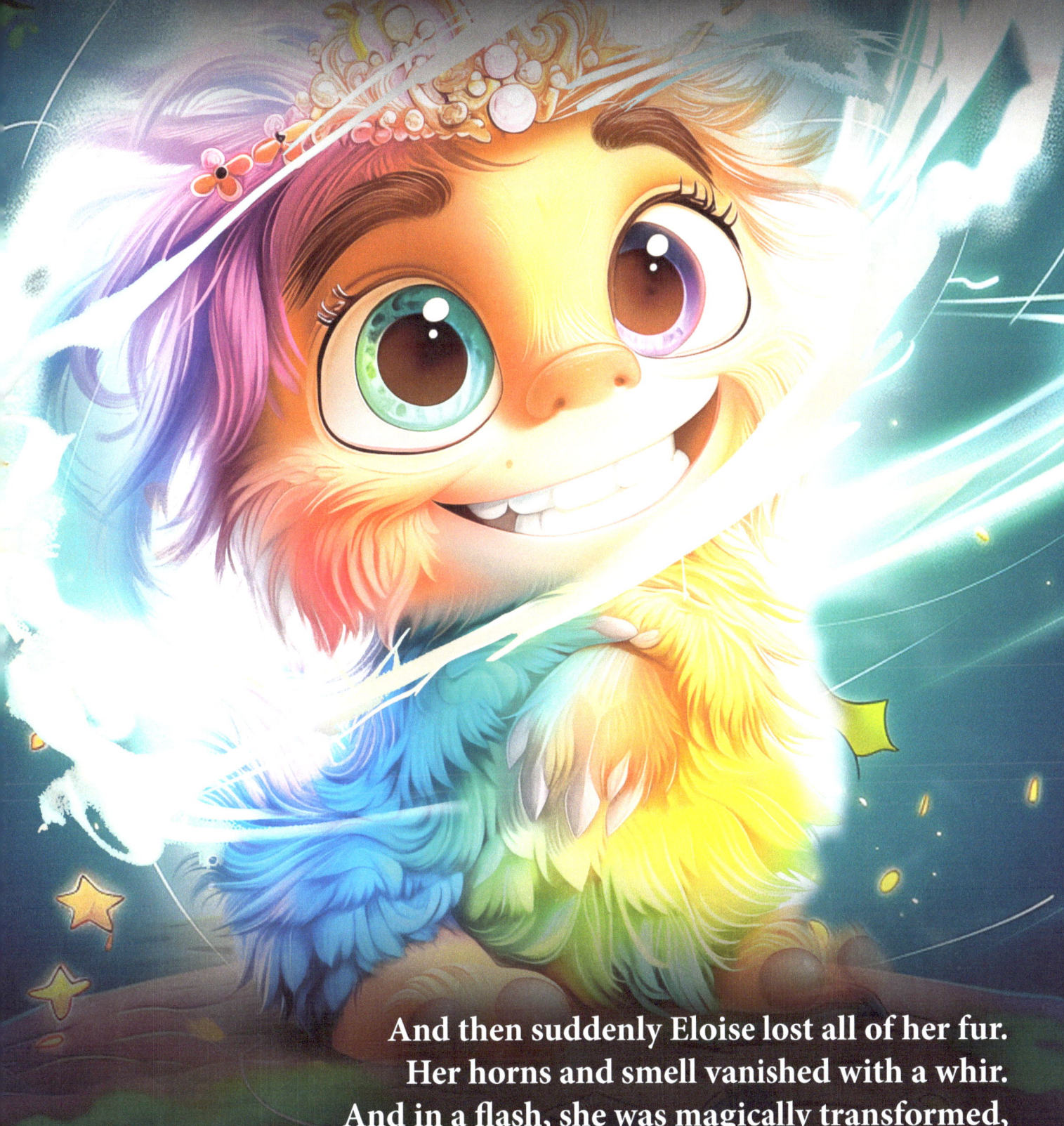

And then suddenly Eloise lost all of her fur.
Her horns and smell vanished with a whir.
And in a flash, she was magically transformed,
Back into the sweet girl she had been once before!

The King smiled and embraced the Princess Eloise,
And gave her her present: her very own Glow Tree!
"We must be slow to anger and slow to fight,
For in meekness is where we will find the light!"

THE END.

"Let every man be swift to hear, slow to speak, slow to wrath: for the wrath of man worketh not the righteousness of God." - James 1:19-20

www.ingramcontent.com/pod-product-compliance
Lightning Source LLC
Chambersburg PA
CBHW041601070526
44586CB00003BA/45